MANDOLIN MUSIC
FOR CHRISTMAS

BY BUTCH BALDASSARI

Music notation by Rob Haines

A recording of the music in this book is now available. The publisher strongly recommends the use of this recording along with the text to insure accuracy of interpretation and ease in learning.

Contents

About the Author

At the forefront of Mandolin music in America today is Nashville's Butch Baldassari. With four solo projects to his credit he has established himself as a creative and diverse instrumentalist. These projects —"What's Doin'," "Old Town," "Evergreen" and "A Day in the Country"— run the gamut from old-time music to traditional bluegrass, new acoustic music and, as documented here, lovely Christmas melodies.

His "World of Mandolin" seminars are held every spring and fall in Nashville. These four-day intensives focus mainly on traditional bluegrass Mandolin styles.

Butch also has been a founding member of bluegrass groups "Weary Hearts" and the 1992 Grammy-nominated "Lonesome Standard Time."

At present Butch is leader of The Nashville Mandolin Ensemble — America's only large touring Mandolin ensemble. Their debut recording, *Plectrasonics,* is on CMH Records.

Nashville Mandolin Ensemble
c/o Butch Baldassari
125 43rd Avenue North
Nashville, TN 37209

God Rest Ye Merry Gentlemen

I recorded this opening piece with a vintage Gibson F-4. I tried to simulate the sound of a small bell ringing by playing very even up and down strokes while keeping the left hand notes fretted for as long as possible. I was going for an even tone and maximum sustain. I doubled up on the melody notes for this overall effect. Be careful to observe slides with your third finger in bars 1, 5, 12, 16, and 23, and that hammer on in bar 21.

Old English Carol
Arr. by Butch Baldassari

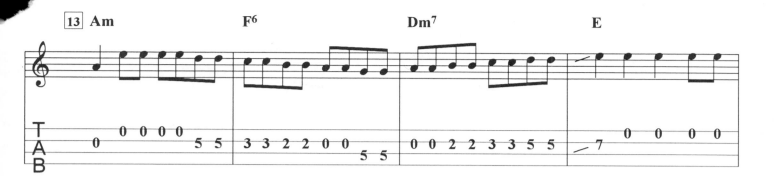

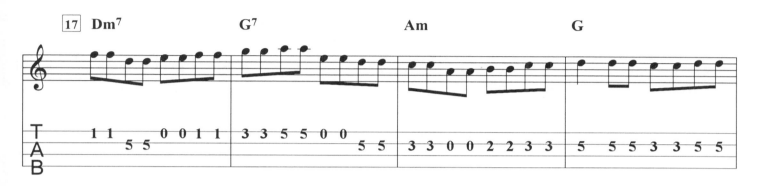

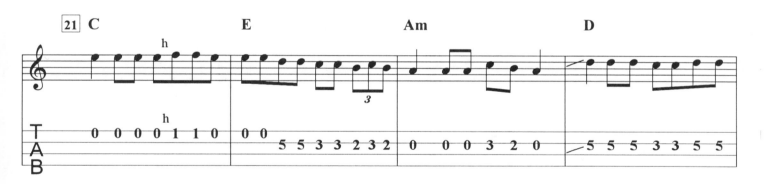

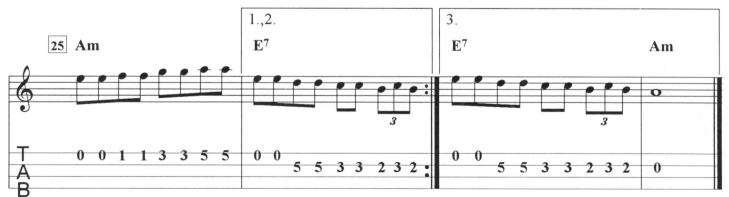

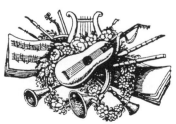

We Three Kings

This is actually part of a two-song medley. I switched from 4/4 to 3/4 Time on this piece. It uses the same approach as *God Rest Ye Merry Gentlemen*, with slides, etc. From bar 9 to the end, I included the lower harmony notes as they were played on the recording. They can be played together, with another Mandolin, melody instrument, or even your guitarist could play them.

John H. Hopkins
Arr. by Butch Baldassari

Mandolin

Verse

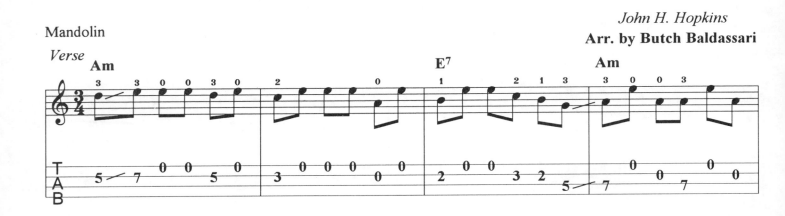

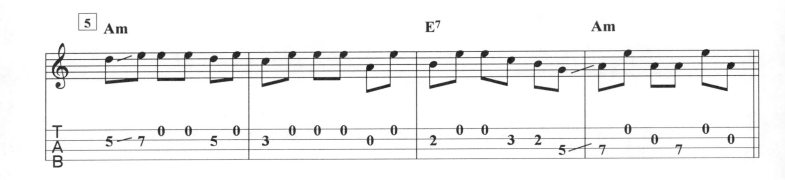

Chorus

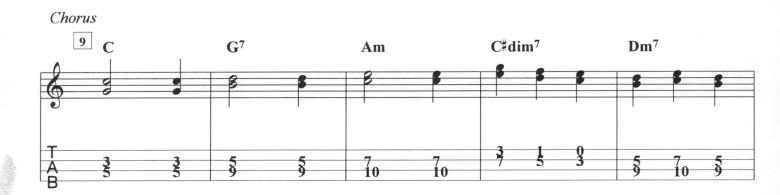

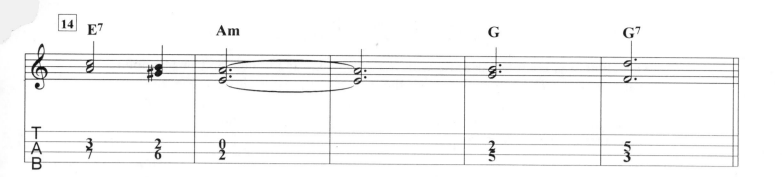

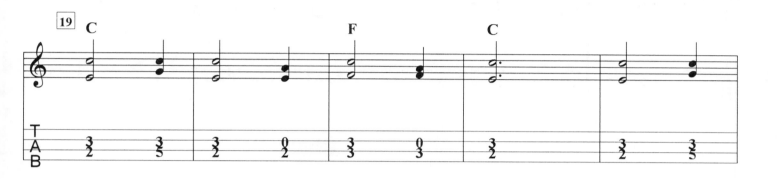

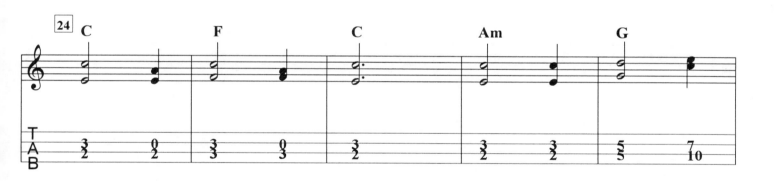

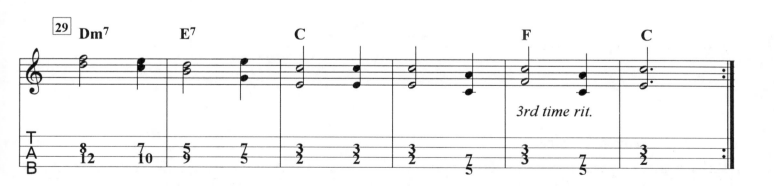

The First Noel

This tune was recorded as a trio with two Mandolins and Mandola. The Mandolin parts are easy. The only option is whether or not to use your pinkie verses an open string which is a common Mandolin dilemma. Also, try all down strokes on the third verse for an even tone. If you don't have a Mandola, the third part can either be Guitar or Octave Mandolin.

Old English Carol
Arr. by Butch Baldassari

Mandolin 1

The First Noel

Mandolin 2

Old English Carol
Arr. by Butch Baldassari

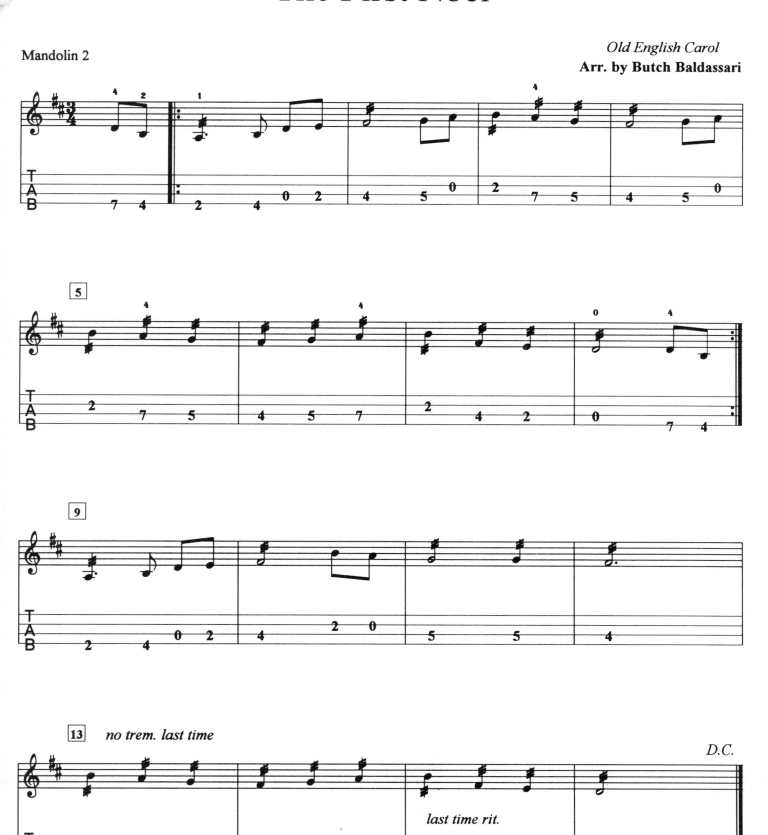

9

The First Noel

Mandola
Guitar
Octave Mandolin

Old English Carol
Arr. by Butch Baldassari

5

9

13 *no trem. last time*

D.C.

Silent Night

On the recording I came in after the Dobro®. That's where we're starting on this page.
Again, I opt for pinkie over open strings. You can try tremolo throughout or try
breaking up the tremolo with down strokes on all of the eighth notes. When it goes
to the key of F, I shift to the second position and use my first finger as a guide.

Mandolin 1

Music by Frans Gruber

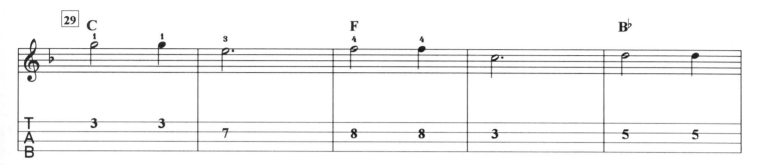

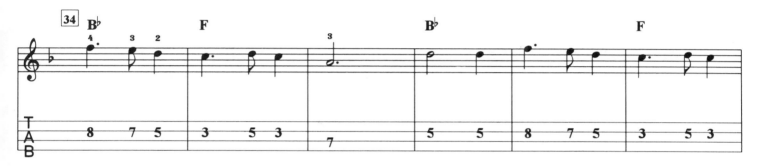

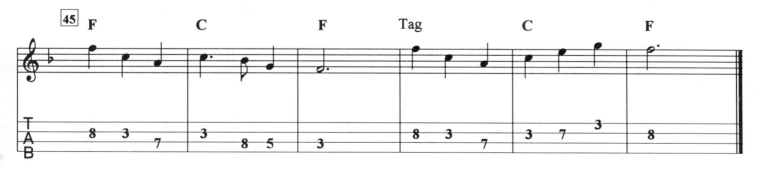

13

Silent Night

Mandolin 2

Mandolin 2 is, again, a lower harmony part and for the most part is played in second position. I've noted the left hand fingers as a guide.

Mandolin 2

Music by Frans Gruber

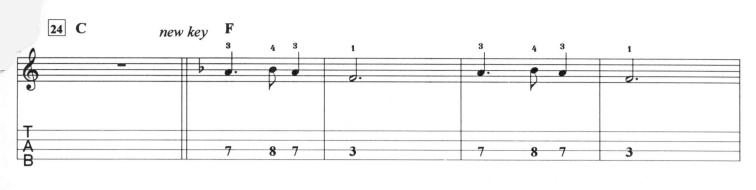

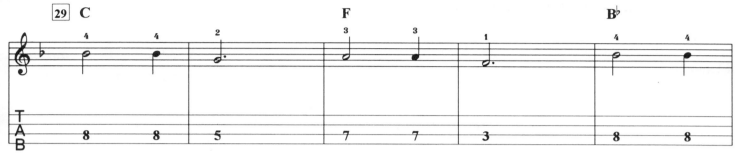

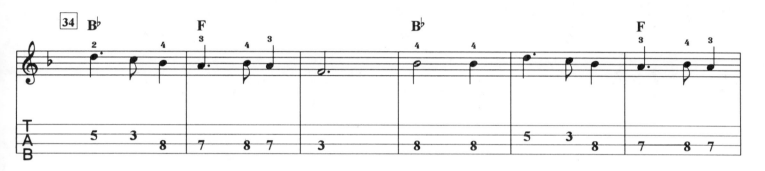

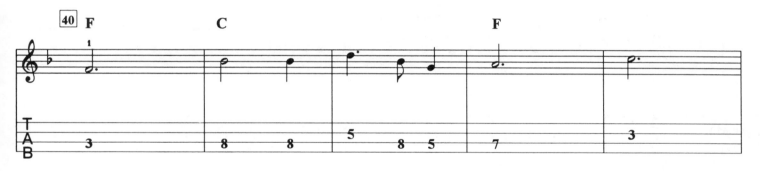

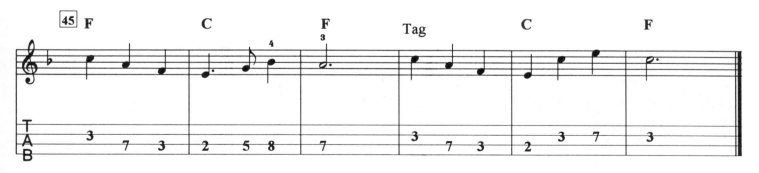

Joy To The World

This was recorded as a mandola solo in the key of C, and here I've used the same fingerings to make it a Mandolin solo in the Key of G. I've notated the first verse, as the other two have slight variations. Once you get the hang of this, you'll see how easy it is to improvise and come up with your own variations. It's all down strokes except the eighth notes that follow the dotted quarters. Go for a big, full sound and even tone across all strings on this one.

Music by G. F. Handel
Arr. by Butch Baldassari

Mandolin Solo

16

What Child Is This

The Evergreen version was done with an octave Mandolin which lent itself to a very lonesome quality that I though this tune needed. Again, down strokes will work throughout. Try up strokes on the eight notes to mix it up. Watch out for the brash sound of the open A notes. Use that pinkie and think *tone*! On the refrain try playing the down strokes between the 14th and 15th fret to produce a flute or bell like tone.

Mandolin
Octave Mandolin

Old English Tune
Arr. by Butch Baldassari

Refrain

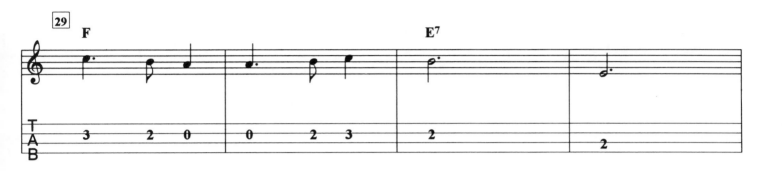

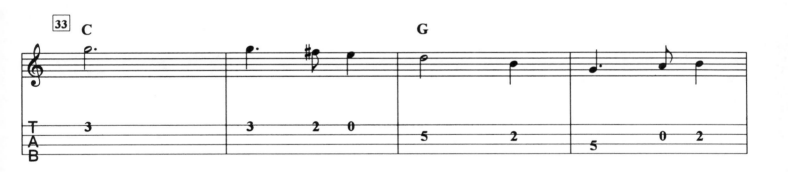

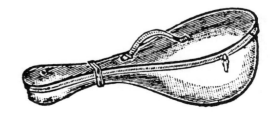

O Little Town Of Bethlehem

A nice kick-off played an octave up from the melody really sets this one up. Try the 15th fret pick attack. Use all down strokes, especially on the intro and you'll hear the difference! On this tune I used a lot of open A's. Watch your attack. There are lots of slides where the 3rd finger is doing most of that work. Observe bars 4, 8, 9 and 19 through 21 in reference to left hand fingerings. The key of F suits the Mandolin well.

Music by Lewis H. Redner
Arr. by Butch Baldassari

Mandolin

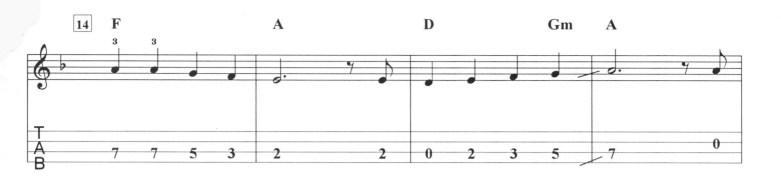

O Holy Night

This number is my favorite piece on Evergreen. I tried to show a lot of contrast in the melody by using tremolo and down strokes. Note that the melody starting at bar 31 to the end is all on the 2nd string. I felt that it really "sung" there and was very consistent sounding. It may feel strange at first to do these shifts; all on one string. Try them because you might enjoy them!

Cantiqué de Noel
French Carol

Mandolin

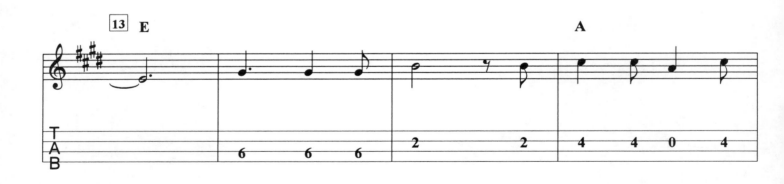

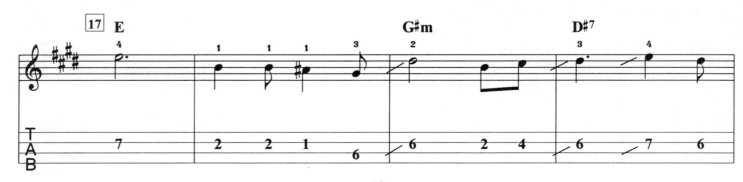

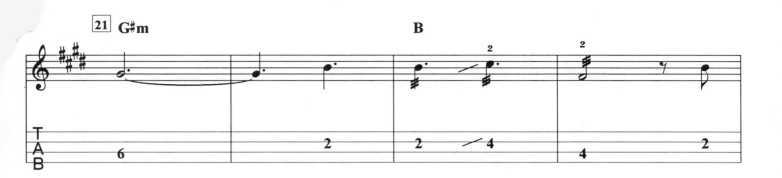

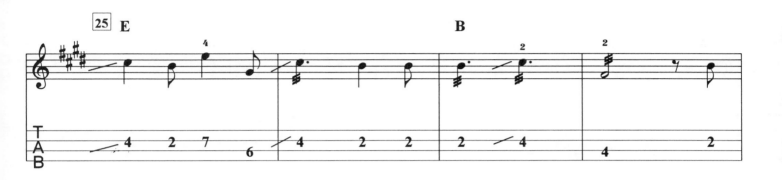

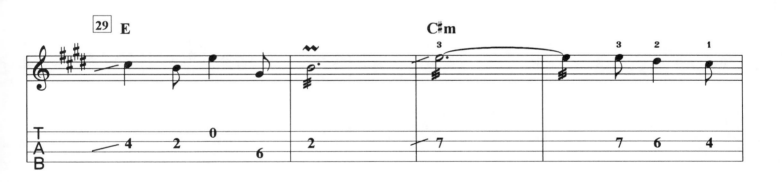

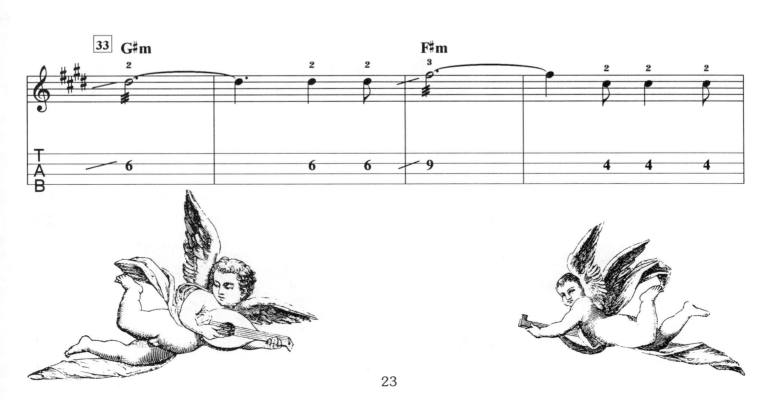

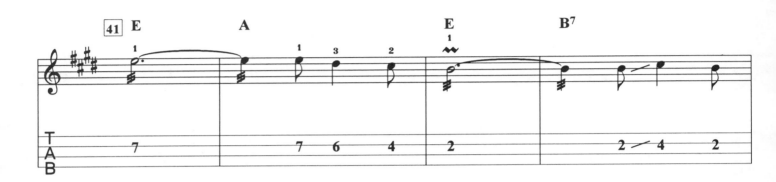

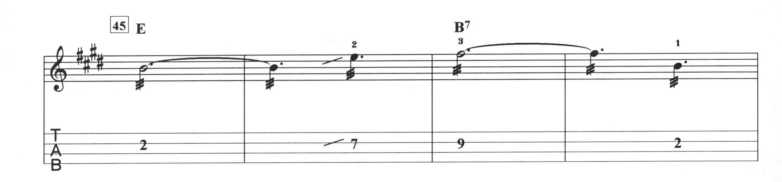

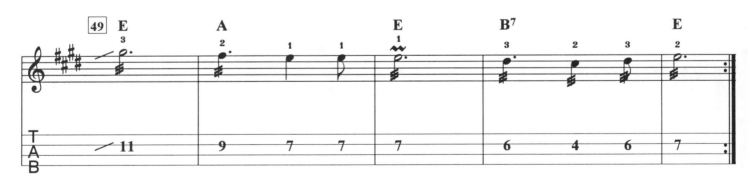

Angels We Have Heard On High

The tune is a pretty straight forward melodic piece. I'm avoiding open strings in bars 13 and 19 to try and keep my sound consistent. Use all down strokes here for sure.

The Westminster Carol
Arr. by Butch Baldassari

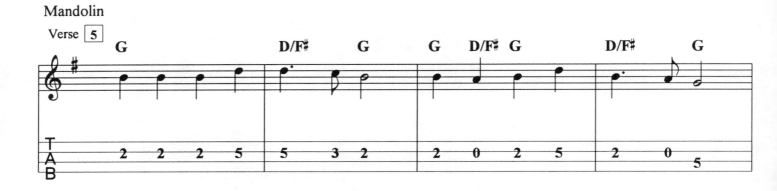

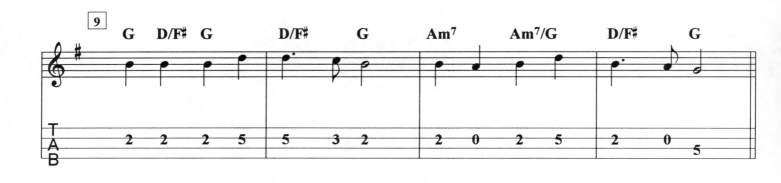

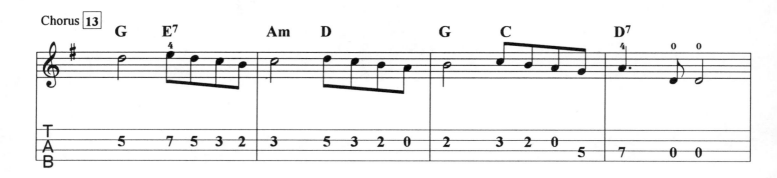

26

Away In A Manger

My version of this old tune was done on the Octave Mandolin but works equally as
well on the Mandolin. This one is a great melody to develop your tone. Try it up
an octave or with tremolo throughout. The Christmas repertoire is a good place to
start to develop a more lyrical quality to your mandolin playing.

Mandolin
Octave Mandolin

Music by Martin Luther
Arr. by Butch Baldassari

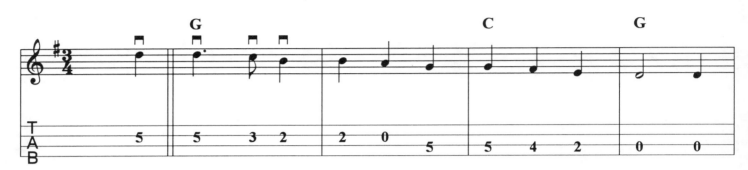

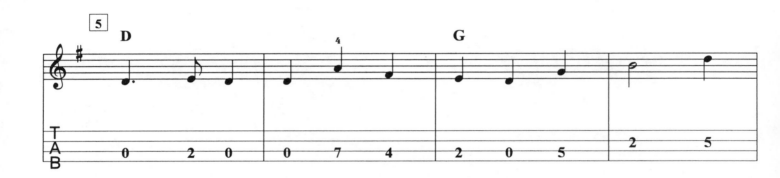

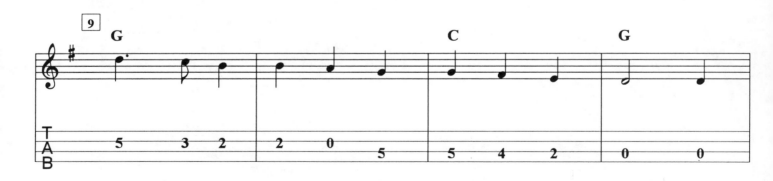

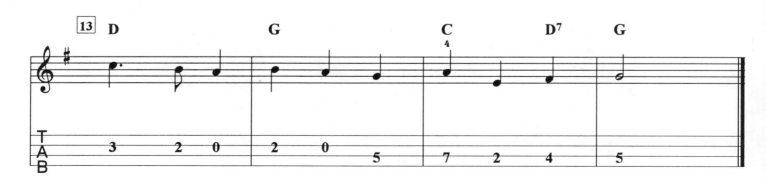

It Came Upon The Midnight Clear

B♭ is another great key for Mandolin! It's all melody, melody, melody, and it's all in the first position. Try to learn the melody an octave up. This tune also works nicely on the Octave Mandolin.

Music by Richard S. Willis
Arr. by Butch Baldassari

Mandolin

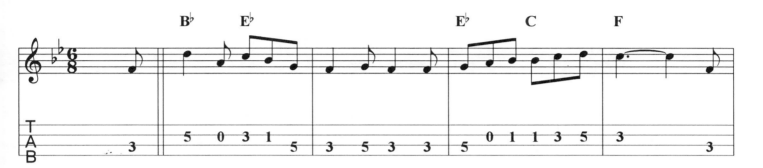

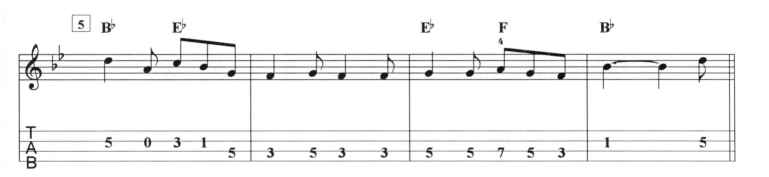

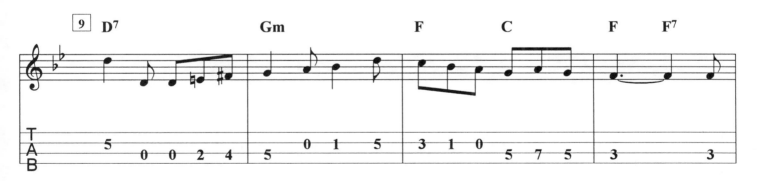

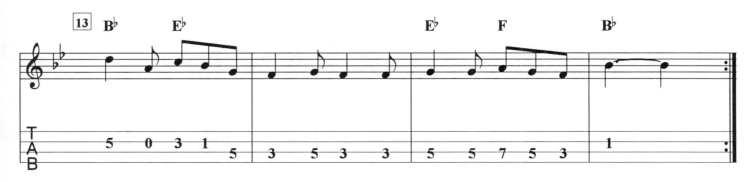

Deck The Halls

This tune was another of my Mandola solos and is included here in the key of G for Mandolin. The first verse is all single notes and each one has got to count. Use down strokes throughout. The second verse is harmonized using alternating pick strokes on the eighth notes, except at the end ritard.

Mandolin
Octave Mandolin

Welsh Carol
Arr. by Butch Baldassari

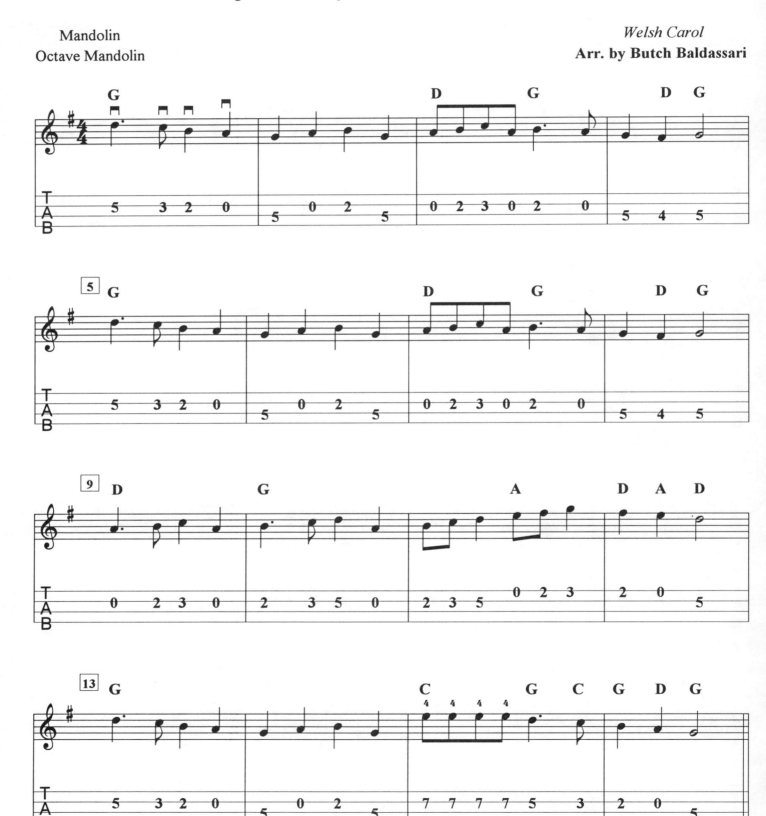

We Wish You A Merry Christmas

I used half of a verse and repeated it over and over. It's a sort of good-bye/Christmas wish and ending to Evergreen. It's very simple all in first position with some basic slides. Have a happy!!!

Traditional English Folk Song
Arr. by Butch Baldassari

Mandolin 1

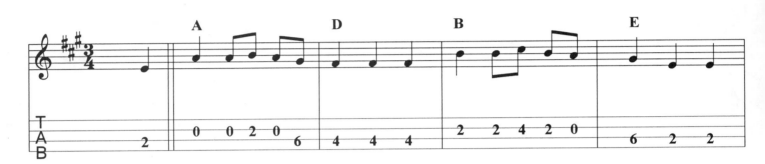